D1441152

2/10

Hawaii

Greetings from HAWAII
The Aloha State

Jim Ollhoff

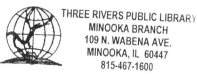

Visit us at
www.abdopublishing.com

Published by ABDO Publishing Company, 8000 West 78th Street, Suite 310, Edina, Minnesota 55439 USA. Copyright ©2010 by Abdo Consulting Group, Inc. International copyrights reserved in all countries. No part of this book may be reproduced in any form without written permission from the publisher. The Checkerboard Library™ is a trademark and logo of ABDO Publishing Company.

Printed in the United States.

Editor: John Hamilton
Graphic Design: Sue Hamilton
Cover Illustration: Neil Klinepier
Cover Photo: iStock Photo
Interior Photo Credits: Alamy, AP Images, Christopher P. Becker, Comstock, Corbis, Emily Kemper, Getty, Granger Collection, iStock Photo, John Webber, Library of Congress, Mile High Maps, Mountain High Maps, One Mile Up, Sue Hamilton, and the White House/Pete Souza.
Statistics: State population statistics taken from 2008 U.S. Census Bureau estimates. City and town population statistics taken from July 1, 2007, U.S. Census Bureau estimates. Land and water area statistics taken from 2000 Census, U.S. Census Bureau.

Manufactured with paper containing at least 10% post-consumer waste

Library of Congress Cataloging-in-Publication Data

Ollhoff, Jim, 1959-
  Hawaii / Jim Ollhoff.
      p. cm. -- (The United States)
  Includes index.
  ISBN 978-1-60453-646-1
  1. Hawaii--Juvenile literature. I. Title.

DU623.25.O45 2009
996.9--dc22
                                          2008051037

Table of Contents

The Aloha State 4

Quick Facts 6

Geography 8

Climate and Weather 12

Plants and Animals 14

History 18

Did You Know? 24

People 26

Cities 30

Transportation 34

Natural Resources 36

Industry 38

Sports 40

Entertainment 42

Timeline 44

Glossary 46

Index 48

The Aloha State

The famous writer Mark Twain said Hawaii was the "loveliest fleet of islands that lies anchored in any ocean." That's a good description of Hawaii. Its eight main islands are a place of unbelievable beauty. It has sandy beaches, lush green forests, tall mountains, and a climate that is warm all year. Hawaii is a rich mix of cultures and people. Many people think Hawaii is a tropical paradise.

Hawaii is called the Aloha State. *Aloha* is a word that means many things. It can mean "hello" or "goodbye." It also means that we should help others. Hawaiians call this the Aloha Spirit. It means to be warm and friendly, and to think about other people and not just about ourselves.

Wailua Falls on the island of Kauai, Hawaii.

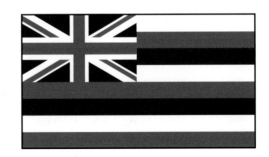

Quick Facts

Name: Possibly from the word "Hawaiki," which may have been an island from which the early inhabitants of Hawaii came.

State Capital: Honolulu

Date of Statehood: August 21, 1959 (50th state)

Population: 1,288,198 (42nd-most populous state)

Area (Total Land and Water): 10,931 square miles (28,311 sq km), 43rd-largest state

Largest City: Honolulu, population 375,571

Nickname: The Aloha State

Motto: *Ua mau ke ea o ka aina i ka pono.* (The life of the land is perpetuated in righteousness.)

State Bird: Nene (Hawaiian Goose)

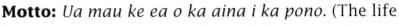

State Flower: Yellow Hibiscus

Black Coral

Kukui Tree

Mauna Kea

Pacific Ocean

Barack Obama

State Gemstone: Black Coral

State Tree: Kukui, also called the Candlenut

State Song: "Hawaii Ponoi" ("Hawaii's Own")

Highest Point: Pu'u Wekiu, Mauna Kea, 13,796 feet (4,205 m)

Lowest Point: Pacific Ocean, 0 feet (0 m)

Average July Temperature: 77°F (25°C)

Record High Temperature: 100°F (38°C) at Pahala, April 27, 1931

Average January Temperature: 71°F (22°C)

Record Low Temperature: 12°F (-11°C) at Mauna Kea, May 17, 1979

Average Annual Precipitation: 400 inches (1,016 cm) in the mountains to less than 10 inches (25 cm) in the lowlands

Number of U.S. Senators: 2

Number of U.S. Representatives: 2

U.S. Presidents Born in Hawaii: Barack Obama

U.S. Postal Service Abbreviation: HI

Geography

The state of Hawaii includes eight major islands. From west to east, the islands are named Niihau, Kauai, Oahu, Molokai, Lanai, Kahoolawe, Maui, and the island of Hawaii. The state of Hawaii also has many tiny islands called islets. Most of the islets are in a huge protected area called the Hawaiian Islands National Wildlife Refuge. The island of Hawaii is the largest of the islands, and is often called the Big Island. Most of the state's people live on Oahu.

Millions of years ago, volcanoes erupted on the floor of the Pacific Ocean. Molten rock spewed up, eventually cooling and forming land. Then, over tens of thousands of years, ocean waves brought plant life, and birds brought seeds. Over time, a wonderful mix of plant and animal life emerged.

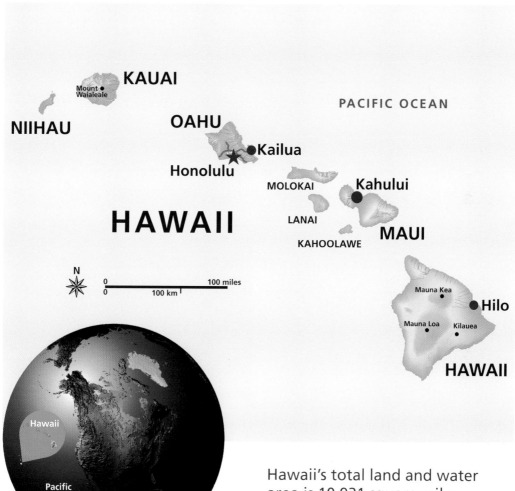

KAUAI

Mount •
Waialeale

PACIFIC OCEAN

NIIHAU

OAHU

●Kailua

★
Honolulu

MOLOKAI

Kahului

HAWAII

LANAI

MAUI

KAHOOLAWE

N

| 0 | | 100 miles |
| 0 | 100 km | |

Mauna Kea •

●Hilo

Mauna Loa •   Kilauea •

HAWAII

Hawaii

Pacific
Ocean

Hawaii's total land and water area is 10,931 square miles (28,311 sq km). It is the 43rd-largest state. The state capital is Honolulu on the island of Oahu.

Hawaii is known for its beautiful sandy beaches. These are caused by strong Pacific Ocean waves carrying sand and rock. This sand and rock grinds against other rock, creating sandy beaches.

Volcanoes are still active on Hawaii. Mauna Loa is one of the largest volcanoes on Earth. Kilauea is a volcano that has a regular lava flow.

There is a large amount of rainfall in the mountains. This makes for gushing waters as it splashes downhill. Over time, the water has eroded the sides of the mountains, creating beautiful grooves and ridges in the mountainsides.

Kauai's Na Pali Coast shows the deep erosion of the mountains.

Important rivers include the Wailuku River on the island of Hawaii and the Anahulu River on Oahu.

Kilauea is one of Hawaii's active volcanoes.

Climate and Weather

The temperature of Hawaii is mild all year round. The temperature ranges from an average low of 72 degrees

Winter snow covers Mauna Kea mountain on the island of Hawaii.

Fahrenheit (22°C) to an average high of 78 degrees Fahrenheit (26°C). Cool ocean winds keep the climate fairly even throughout the seasons. In high mountain areas, it can be cooler. On mountaintops in winter, there can even be snow.

Hawaii's rainfall varies a lot. Mount Waialeale, on the island of Kauai, receives an average of 444 inches (1,128 cm) of rain per year. This area is sometimes called the wettest place on Earth. On the island of Hawaii, an area called Kawaihae gets only about 9 inches (23 cm) of rain per year.

Mount Waialeale is sometimes called the wettest place on Earth.

Plants and Animals

There are more than 2,500 different plants that are native to Hawaii. There are also many kinds of plants that have been brought to the islands by humans. Many plants have become extinct in Hawaii.

When the first humans came to Hawaii, they brought with them many kinds of fruits and roots. These included coconut, sweet potato, banana, sugarcane, breadfruit, and taro. They also brought seeds to plant trees, which included Malay apple, paper mulberry, and kukui, which is the state tree.

When the Europeans and Americans began to settle in Hawaii in the 1800s, they brought many other trees and plants. These included pine, mesquite, and eucalyptus. They also brought many kinds of flowers.

Taro is a plant grown in Hawaii and other tropical locations. In its raw form, it is poisonous. Once cooked or soaked overnight in cold water, it can be safely eaten. Taro is used to make the traditional Hawaiian dish of poi.

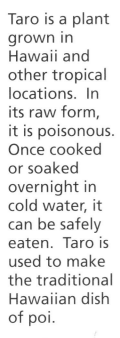

Forests cover almost half of Hawaii. Grassy areas and pasture cover another 25 percent of the land area. Common trees include the hala, ohia, and koa.

The only mammals known to be native to Hawaii are the hoary bat and the Hawaiian monk seal. Humans brought other animals to Hawaii. They include mongoose, rats, deer, and goats. Farmers raise cattle, sheep, and pigs. Frogs, toads, geckos, turtles, and lizards are common reptiles and amphibians.

Birds are plentiful in Hawaii. Honeycreeper, elepaio, apapane, Hawaiian hawk, sparrow, cardinal, and dove are common. Along the ocean coast are tern, shearwater, petrel, and frigate birds.

Ocean waters around Hawaii teem with fish. More than 600 kinds of fish swim around the islands. Marlin, swordfish, skipjack, snapper, mackerel, and tuna can be found in the deep waters.

Hoary bats are native to Hawaii.

Scarlet Honeycreeper

Lizard on Ginger Blossom

Sea Turtle

History

The first people came to Hawaii sometime between 300 AD and 700 AD. They came by boat from the Marquesas Islands. The Marquesas Islands are about 2,000 miles (3,219 km) south of Hawaii.

About 1000 AD, more settlers arrived. These people came from the island of Tahiti. The early people of Hawaii

A Hawaiian warrior.

fished and farmed. They raised chickens and pigs. Their main crop was taro, a root grown in watery fields. Taro was baked and then ground into a food called poi.

Carved wooden figures known as tikis represent Hawaiian gods. These stand in the Pu`uhonau o Honaunau National Historic Park in Hawaii.

Priests taught the people to believe in many gods. They had many religious rules to follow. Chiefs of various groups fought with each other over land and resources.

In 1778, the British explorer Captain James Cook landed on the island of Kauai. He named the land "the Sandwich Islands." Captain Cook wanted to honor the man who funded the expedition, John Montagu, the fourth Earl of Sandwich. Later, the name "Sandwich Islands" became used less and less as the United States grew in influence.

Captain Cook returned to Hawaii in 1779. This time, his relations with the native Hawaiians turned sour. Captain Cook died in a battle with them.

Captain Cook died in a battle with Hawaiians on February 14, 1779.

European settlers began to move to Hawaii soon afterward. A great many native Hawaiians died from the new settlers' European diseases.

Throughout most of Hawaii's history, there were many kingdoms, each with its own chief. In the years 1791 to 1810, King Kamehameha united all the warring tribes. They finally became one kingdom.

Kamehameha I was king of the Hawaiian islands from 1810–1819. He is often called Kamehameha the Great for uniting all the islands.

In 1820, the first Christian missionaries arrived. This continued to make the people of Hawaii more like people in the United States. They began to lose some of their traditional Hawaiian culture. Companies began to grow sugar. Since the large sugar plantations needed many workers, companies brought in workers from Japan and China.

Sanford Dole was president of the Republic of Hawaii and later the first governor of the Territory of Hawaii.

Throughout the 1800s, there was tension between the traditional Hawaiian culture and the influence of the United States. United States representatives and colonists seized control of the islands in 1893. The new Hawaii government created the Republic of Hawaii in 1894, with Sanford Dole as its president. In 1898, Hawaii became an official territory of the United States.

The Japanese attack on Pearl Harbor.

In the late 1930s, problems grew between Japan and the United States. Japan wanted to expand its control. On December 7, 1941, Japanese planes attacked the military base at Pearl Harbor on the island of Oahu. The attack destroyed many ships and planes. More than 2,300 American lives were lost. The Japanese military hoped the attack would cripple the United States. It did not. An angry United States government quickly declared war on Japan, and so began the U.S. involvement in World War II.

In 1959, Hawaii became the 50th state of the United States. In the years following, agriculture became less important. Tourism became the most important part of Hawaii's economy.

Did You Know?

- The island of Hawaii is the biggest of the Hawaiian islands. More than 35 percent of the world's macadamia nuts are grown in Hawaii.

- One of the world's largest inactive volcanoes, Haleakala Crater, is on the island of Maui.

- The island of Kauai has chickens that run wild on the island.

- The island of Molokai has the highest cliffs, the biggest beach, and the longest waterfall in Hawaii.

- The island of Niihau is mostly privately owned. The biggest business is raising livestock.

- The island of Oahu has the biggest population. More than 100 famous beaches are on Oahu. Waikiki Beach is the most famous.

- The island of Lanai was once home to the largest pineapple plantation in the world.

- The island of Kahoolawe is off-limits to people. The United States military once used it for target practice, and so there is a danger of unexploded bombs on the island. The military and Hawaii are working to clean the island.

People

Barack Obama (1961–) was born and grew up in Hawaii. His mother was from Kansas, and his father was from Kenya, Africa. Obama graduated from Columbia University in New York and Harvard Law School in Massachusetts. He became the first African American president of the *Harvard Law Review*, a student-run journal. After graduation, he moved to Chicago, Illinois, where he worked to help people who had lost their jobs. Obama became a U.S. senator from Illinois in 2005, helping pass important tax and health care laws. On January 20, 2009, Obama was sworn in as the 44th president of the United States.

 **Kamehameha I** (1758?–1819) was the first king of the Kingdom of Hawaii. In the past, there were many kingdoms in Hawaii, and a lot of fighting between the kingdoms. Partly through treaties, and partly through warfare, he became the head of all the kingdoms in 1810. He made deals with other countries and collected money from their ships. He worked to keep Hawaiian culture alive.

 **Liliuokalani** (1838–1917) was the last queen of the Kingdom of Hawaii. She took the throne in 1891. She organized schools for children and visited other countries. She didn't want Hawaii taken over by the United States. This angered many Americans living in Hawaii. They seized power. She surrendered to avoid warfare, and spent years under arrest. She later wrote a book about her experiences called *Hawaii's Story by Hawaii's Queen*.

Father Damien (1840–1889) was a Catholic priest who devoted his life to helping Hawaiian people who had a skin disease called leprosy. His given name was Jozef de Veuster, and he was born in Belgium. He went to Hawaii as a missionary. He arrived there in 1864.

Leprosy was a dangerous disease in those days. People with leprosy were sent to a special settlement on the island of Molokai so they wouldn't infect others. Father Damien volunteered to help take charge of the village of lepers. He worked as a priest, a doctor, and a teacher, and improved water and food supplies. He eventually contracted leprosy in 1884, and died five years later. In 2009, the Catholic church made Father Damien a saint.

Don Ho (1930–2007) was a famous singer and entertainer. He made music that reminded people of Hawaii. He was born in Honolulu, and moved to Kaneohe. He took a job singing in a nightclub. People came from all over to hear him sing. He began to play for bigger audiences. He sold many records, and was a frequent guest on TV shows. He traveled all over the United States, bringing Hawaiian music to the mainland.

Cities

Honolulu is on the southeast side of the island of Oahu. The city's population is 375,571. People have been living in the Honolulu area since about 1200 AD, and possibly much earlier. In 1809, King Kamehameha I moved his royal court to the area

Diamond Head, a volcanic crater, overlooks Honolulu.

of Honolulu. Most of the air and ship traffic that comes to Hawaii comes through Honolulu. Waikiki is a famous tourist area in the city. It has many shops and beautiful beaches. Honolulu is the home to several universities, including the University of Hawaii at Manoa.

Kailua is on the east side of the island of Oahu. It is about 12 miles (19 km) north and east of Honolulu. Its population is 36,513. The name of the city comes from two words that mean "two seas." This is because there are two lagoons separated by a peninsula. People have been living in the area for about 1,500 years. Kailua Beach is a beautiful beach that promotes heavy tourism.

The beautiful Kailua Beach is one of the best beaches in the world.

Hilo sits along Hilo Bay on the island of Hawaii. It is the largest settlement on the island of Hawaii, with a population of more than 40,000. People settled in the area about 1100 AD, taking up farming and fishing. The city is the home to many museums. The University of Hawaii has a campus at Hilo.

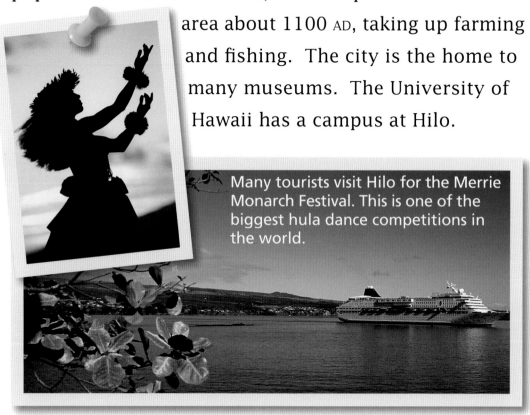

Many tourists visit Hilo for the Merrie Monarch Festival. This is one of the biggest hula dance competitions in the world.

Kahului is on the north coast of the island of Maui. Beginning in the late 1800s, the area was a center for sugar production. After World War II, the city expanded with an airport and many businesses. Today, the population is more than 20,000. The University of Hawaii has a campus in this city.

Fields of sugar cane surround a sugar mill in Kahului, Maui.

Transportation

The only interstate highways in Hawaii are on the island of Oahu. Interstate H1 is on the south side of the island. Interstate H2 goes north and south, and H3 goes east and west. There are about 4,280 miles (6,888 km) of roads in Hawaii.

Ocean transportation is very important. Honolulu, on the island of Oahu, is the most important harbor. Ships take goods out of Hawaii to sell in the United States or other countries, and deliver imported goods.

Honolulu Harbor is a busy place. Ships take goods to and from many countries.

More than 21 million people traveled through Honolulu International Airport in 2007.

Most of the visitors to Hawaii come to Honolulu International Airport. This airport is one of the busiest airports in the nation. From there, tourists can fly to most of the other islands, which have smaller airports.

Natural Resources

James Dole created the first pineapple plantation in Oahu in 1901. Today, about 33 percent of the world's pineapple crop comes from Hawaii.

There are more than 7,000 farms in Hawaii. Pineapple and sugarcane are the most valuable crops. Macadamia nuts are also grown in Hawaii. These are sent to the mainland United States and other countries. Some other fruits and vegetables are grown, but mainly for Hawaiians. Hawaii is working to grow more kinds of crops. Papaya, banana, guava, and passion fruit farming are growing in importance.

There are many large cattle and hog ranches. Chickens and dairy cows are raised in some places. There is some commercial fishing. Much of the catch is tuna, mostly skipjack tuna and yellowfin tuna.

There are no mineral deposits or precious gems in Hawaii. Crushed stone, sand, and gravel are quarried.

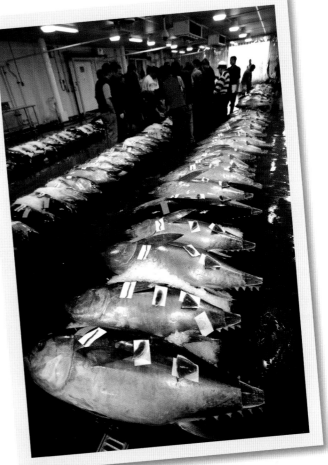

Yellowfin tuna sold at a fish auction in Oahu, Hawaii. Many will go to restaurants, where they are served grilled or raw. Yellowfin are also known as ahi tuna.

Industry

Agriculture is a very small part of Hawaii's economy. Only about two percent of the money in the state economy is from agriculture.

There are many manufacturing plants. Factories make food products, like canned pineapple, canned fish, and sugar. Other factories make clothing or cement.

Science and research are becoming increasingly important. One of the biggest telescopes in the world is in Hawaii.

Astronomers view the skies from the Keck Observatory on the island of Hawaii. The observatory is on the top of Mauna Kea, an extinct volcano.

The United States government puts a lot of money into Hawaii's economy. This is mostly because of large military bases in the state.

The biggest part of Hawaii's economy is tourism. Many jobs are in the service industry. These include jobs in hotels and restaurants. About 7 million people visit Hawaii each year, putting more than $10 billion into the economy.

Hawaii has been a popular place to visit for many decades. A great number of local people work as musicians, dancers, singers, cooks, waiters, and housekeepers in the state's many motels, hotels, and restaurants.

Sports

Hawaii has no professional sports teams. However, the National Football League has played the Pro Bowl in Honolulu for many years. Professional golfers play in Hawaii. Some college teams play

University of Hawaii's "Valli the Warrior" cheers during the Hawaii Bowl at Aloha Stadium.

championships in the state, such as the Hawaii Bowl in December. The World Ironman Triathlon Championship is held in Hawaii. The Honolulu Marathon is held in December each year, drawing more than 20,000 runners.

Surfing is very popular in Hawaii. There are hundreds of surf spots off the shores of the Hawaiian islands. Surfing competitions are held in the state, many at Makaha Beach on the island of Oahu.

Hawaii's mild climate makes it a great place for many outdoor activities. Hiking in the mountains, golf, tennis, camping, swimming, and diving are all popular.

Big-wave surfers catch a wave at Oahu's Waimea Bay Beach Park in Haleiwa, Hawaii. Some waves may reach heights of 40 feet (12 m).

Entertainment

Hawaii is a mix of many different cultures. Hawaiians are very interested in museums and arts that highlight culture. The Honolulu Academy of Arts is sometimes called the most beautiful museum in the world.

A girl plays a ukulele.

The original Hawaiian culture remains, and is becoming stronger again in the islands. Asian cultures, particularly Japanese, are present. Many people can trace their history to New England and Europe.

One famous kind of recreation is the Hawaiian luau. It is a feast of traditional Hawaiian food. Native dancers often perform in traditional clothing to the music of ukuleles.

There are hundreds of places to visit in Hawaii. There are two national parks. Hawaii Volcanoes National Park is on the island of Hawaii. Haleakala National Park is on the island of Maui.

Scientists and tourists come to see the amazing eruptions and lava flows at Hawaii Volcanoes National Park.

Timeline

300 to 700—The first people come to Hawaii from the Marquesas Islands.

About 1000—More settlers arrive in Hawaii from Tahiti.

1778—British explorer Captain James Cook lands in Hawaii.

King Kamehameha I

1791 to 1810—King Kamehameha I unites all the kingdoms into one.

1820—The first Christian missionaries arrive on the islands.

Queen Liliuokalani

1893—United States representatives and colonists seize control of the islands. Queen Liliuokalani surrenders.

1898—Hawaii becomes an official territory of the United States. Sanford Dole becomes president of the territory.

1941—The Japanese military attacks the U.S. military base at Pearl Harbor. The United States enters World War II.

1959—Hawaii becomes the 50th state of the United States.

2009—Hawaii-native Barack Obama becomes the 44th president of the United States.

Glossary

Islet—A tiny island.

Leprosy—A disease that causes disfiguring skin sores, nerve damage, and muscle weakness. People with the disease are known as lepers. A person with the disease may give it to another person. Because of this, people with the disease were often sent to live in specific places with other lepers. For example, the island of Molokai once had a leper colony. Today, medicines exist to treat leprosy, so isolating infected people is not necessary.

Luau—A traditional Hawaiian feast.

Marquesas Islands—Islands about 2,000 miles (3,219 km) south of Hawaii, homeland of the first Hawaiian settlers.

Missionary—A person sent on a mission to teach a specific religion or to help people in their everyday lives.

New England—An area of the United States that refers to the states of Connecticut, Maine, Massachusetts, New Hampshire, Rhode Island, and Vermont. People from this area are often called New Englanders.

Poi—A native Hawaiian food made by mixing the taro root with water, cooking it, then pounding the taro into a paste. Poi may be eaten right away or allowed to sit for several days for a more sour flavor.

Tahiti—An island south of Hawaii, and east of Australia. People from Tahiti helped to settle Hawaii.

Taro—A root that was an important food source for the early people of Hawaii.

Ukulele—A four-stringed musical instrument shaped like a small guitar. It is used in many popular Hawaiian tunes.

World War II—A conflict across the world, lasting from 1939-1945. The United States entered the war in December 1941, after Pearl Harbor was bombed by the Japanese military.

Index

A
Africa 26
Anahulu River 10

B
Belgium 28
Big Island (*See* Hawaii, island of)

C
Catholic church 28
Chicago, IL 26
China 22
Columbia University 26
Cook, James 20

D
Damien, Father 28
Dole, Sanford 22

E
Earth 10, 13
Europe 42

H
Haleakala Crater 24
Haleakala National Park 43
Harvard Law Review 26
Harvard Law School 26
Hawaii, island of 8, 10, 13, 24, 32, 43
Hawaii, Kingdom of 27

Hawaii, Republic of 22
Hawaii Bowl 40
Hawaii Volcanoes National Park 43
Hawaiian Islands National Wildlife Refuge 8
Hawaii's Story by Hawaii's Queen 27
Hilo, HI 32
Hilo Bay 32
Ho, Don 29
Honolulu, HI 29, 30, 31, 34, 40
Honolulu Academy of Arts 42
Honolulu International Airport 35
Honolulu Marathon 40

I
Illinois 26

J
Japan 22, 23

K
Kahoolawe, island of 8, 25
Kahului, HI 33
Kailua, HI 31
Kailua Beach 31
Kamehameha I 21, 27, 30

Kaneohe, HI 29
Kansas 26
Kauai, island of 8, 13, 20, 24
Kawaihae, HI 13
Kenya, Africa 26
Kilauea 10

L
Lanai, island of 8, 25
Liliuokalani 27

M
Makaha Beach 41
Manoa, HI 30
Marquesas Islands 18
Massachusetts 26
Maui, island of 8, 24, 33, 43
Mauna Loa 10
Molokai, island of 8, 24, 28
Montagu, John 20

N
National Football League 40
New England 42
New York 26
Niihau, island of 8, 25

O
Oahu, island of 8, 10, 23, 25, 30, 31, 34, 41
Obama, Barack 26

P
Pacific Ocean 8, 10
Pearl Harbor 23
Pro Bowl 40

S
Sandwich, Earl of 20
Sandwich Islands 20

T
Tahiti 18
Twain, Mark 4

U
United States 20, 22, 23, 25, 26, 27, 29, 34, 36, 39
University of Hawaii 30, 32, 33

V
Veuster, Jozef de 28

W
Waialeale, Mount 13
Waikiki 30
Waikiki Beach 25
Wailuku River 10
World Ironman Triathlon Championship 40
World War II 23, 33